# MISS KITTY'S GUIDE

# TO HEALTHY LIVING

## Advice from an Experienced Cat

WRITTEN BY

**MISS KITTY and** JONNY KATZ

WITH SPECIAL THANKS TO
MERIDITH BERK
FOR HER DESIGN ADVICE AND
INFINITESIMAL CONTRIBUTION
TO THIS WORK

*Dear Reader,*

*I've been used. A few months ago, my cat, Miss Kitty related several pieces of advice she had for humans to help them lead better and healthier lives. These ideas sounded good to me and I told her so. Then I made a big mistake. I mentioned she should put her ideas into a book.*

*As you know, not only do cats not have thumbs, but many do not even know how to type.*

*I agreed to put together a little book for her. I thought it would be short and quick. Nope. Miss Kitty got carried away, as she always does, and before I knew it, she was inviting her friends to contribute and even trying her paw at poetry.*

*One thing led to another and I've spent the last two months as the typing and design slave of Miss Kitty and her friends.*

*For better or for worse here is, "Miss Kitty's Guide to Healthy Living."*

*I hope you enjoy it as much as I enjoyed finishing it.*

*Jonny K.*

"Part of any Successful Life: The Ability to Catch a Nap... Any Time, Any Where."

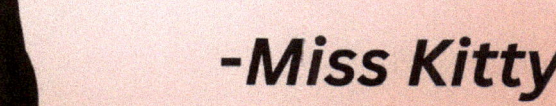

-Miss Kitty

## Choose Words Wisely

"You may say a cat uses good grammar.
Well, a cat does – but you let a cat get
excited once; you let a cat get to pulling
fur with another cat on a shed, nights,
and you'll hear grammar that will give
you the lockjaw. Ignorant people think
it's the noise which fighting cats
make that is so aggravating, but it ain't
so; it's the sickening grammar they use"
- Mark Twain (1835-1910)

Always say what you mean;
people judge us by our words
not just our actions. (More's the pity)

# A Job to Do

"Don't scratch this and don't scratch that
Leave the couch alone
You sink your claws in everything
You're ruining our home"

"These words float by me like the breeze
I have a job to do
To make this house look like a home
I can't leave that to you."

"Good Advice Can
Come From
Strange Places.
Listen.
It Never Hurts to
Hear Another
Point of View."

*-The Gang of Three*

"When I see your naked feet,

All I think is, what a treat.

To pounce, to nip, to have some fun,

Such joy to think the night's begun."

-Miss Kitty

*Set Time Aside Each Day For Play*

"Don't Worry
If Your
Special Person
Leaves
The House.
She'll Be Back
Soon -
Possibly
With Snacks."

-Harold
'The Nervous Optimist'

*From the Desk of*
*Miss Kitty*

*Dearest Human,*

*"I admit there are times when I've taken advice from a dog.*

*Months ago, when I was having some trouble pulling out a houseplant, a puppy friend told me, "If you can't eat it or play with it, just pee on the darned thing and walk away."*

*This works great for dogs and almost as well for cats, but unfortunately for you, my dear humans, this may get you into trouble. So, perhaps it would be best to simply imagine peeing on the object of your disfavor and walk on by."*

*Miss Kitty*

"Never Completely
Trust A Spoon...
In Fact, I Strongly
Recommend
Giving Up Utensils
Entirely."

-Mr. Thumbs

"As My Friend
Nora, The Piano Player
Once Told Me, 'A Little
Music Can Always
Improve Your Spirits.'"

-*Miss Kitty*

"I believe cats to be spirits come to earth.

A cat, I am sure, could walk on a cloud

without coming through."

- Jules Verne

"How right he is!" – Miss Kitty

"I think the cloud business is a bit much."

- Jonny

"There's Nothing
Quite Like Keeping A
Diary To Make You
Realize How Wonderful
You Really Are."

-Miss Kitty

"My Friend
*Fluffy Paws 'The Impaler'*
Knows How to
Greet a Dentist.
You Might Want to Try This
Yourself Just For Fun."

-*Miss Kitty*

# Ode to a Mouse Hole

I sit
I stare
I wait
You're mine

- Patience and Penny Parker

**Patience is Frequently Rewarded**

"Don't Smoke.
It Isn't As Cool As It Used To Be.
Besides, You Might
Burn Off Your Whiskers.
That Happened to My
Uncle Horace Ragbottom
and He Ended Up With His
Head Stuck in a Tiny Mouse Hole
For Hours."

*-Penny "The Duchess" Ragbottom*

"Choose Your Friends Wisely.
If You Don't,
It Could Ruin Your Game."

-*Miss Kitty*

"Everybody Loves
Music.
What Some Call
Caterwauling,
Others Call
A Kitty Choir."

*- Oscar 'The Philosopher'
Garcia*

"What greater gift than the

love of a cat."

- Charles Dickens

"Maybe a new car?" – Jonny

"Heathen!" – Miss Kitty

"Look Cute.
Nobody Will Ever
Suspect You
Ate the Plant!"
-Delilah Furzinski

"Looking For Some
Alone Time?
Stare Meaningfully
At Any Intruder
And They Will
Bow Before
Your Godliness."

-Miss Kitty

"Don't Work So Hard;
Take a Break
From the Computer.
Go Out And Buy Some Toys
for the Cat."

*-Frederick*

"A Big-Eyed Innocent
Look Is
The Ultimate Denial"

-Lucy "Cuddles" Adams

A fine tale.

(ATKINS) SERIES 4.

"There's Nothing
Quite Like A
Good Book
to Lift The Spirits".

-Clara

Don't Let This
Picture Fool You.
They Don't Sell  Kittens
At Costco.
(More's The Pity.)

"Climbing to The
Top Can Be
The Easy Part.
Sometimes It's
Harder to Find Your Way
Back Down."

*-Charlie 'The
Adventurer' Harris*

"Dream Big.
In Some Lifetime,
You Too,
May Get To Be A Cat."

*-Jake 'The Optimist'
De La Mancha*

"Don't Dance With
This Guy (Or Anyone
Who Looks Like Him).
He's way Too Handsy."

*-Ginger  "Twinkle Toes"
Rogers*

"Trust Me.
There Is Such A Thing
As Too Much Caffeine.
This is my Aunt Peaches
After Her 5th Espresso.
Don't Let This Happen to
You. "

*-Miss Kitty*

"Know When You're Happy
and Revel In It."

-Snuggles Romanoff

"I Forget What I Was
Going To Tell You, But I
know It Was Important."

-Furry Potter

**"There's Nothing Quite
Like Getting Together
With Friends
And Having A Good Laugh."**

*-Tom "Good Times" Jones*

"Even If You're Feeling
Weak As A Kitten Now,
It Won't Be Long Before You're
Taking On The Lions Again."

-Calamity Chloe

"After a Long Day,
I Like to Relax
By Going Bowling."

-Sleepytime Sally

"We All Behave
A Little Badly At Times.
Don't Worry About It.
Have some fun."

*-Whitey and Snowflake*

"Don't Overdo
That Exercise Stuff.
If You Need To Rest,
You Need To Rest."

*-Sleepy Boy*

"Once in a While,
We All Need To Go
A Little Wild."

-Mischief and
Stinker

# LITTLE SURPRISES

To help my human wake up fast
and give her lots of fun,
I share some little treats
that keep her on the run.

A tiny mouse, a big fat rat
A bird, a lizard too
So many things that I can share
That make her happy too.

The right surprise is all it takes
To make her cry out loud,
And shriek and run around the house
I know I make her proud.

-Miss Kitty

*Friends Enjoy Receiving
Little Surprises*

"If You Think You're Trapped, You Might Just Have To Look At Things From A Different Angle."

-Katnip Carlisle

"I'm Pretending To Be
A Bar Of Soap;
Please Don't
Give Me Away."

-*Little Lady*

"I Think Coffee Tastes
Better When You
Drink Out Of Someone
Else's Cup.
Try It. It's Fun."

-Bartholemew

Be Prepared When You
Sign Up For Ancestry.com
You May Find Some
Strange Characters
In Your Family Tree.

"Posture
Isn't Everything"

-Mittens

## CAT LOVERS

**Elizabeth Taylor**
**Florence Nightingale**
**Mark Twain**
**Ernest Hemingway**
**Sir Isaac Newton**
**Emily Bronte**
**Stephen King**
**Clara Barton**
**Edgar Allan Poe**
**Abraham Lincoln**
**Neil Gaiman**
**T.S. Eliot**
**Jack Kerouac**
**Charles Dickens**

**Notice how intelligent and creative these cat lovers are.**

**Compare with cat haters.**

# CAT HATERS

**Benito Mussolini**
**Adolf Hitler**
**Napoleon Bonaparte**
**Genghis Khan**
**Henry III of France**
**King Louis XIV**
**Pope Gregory IX**
**Julius Caesar**

"Beware of people who dislike cats."
– Irish Saying

Jonny insists this comparison is a bit
one-sided.

I leave that decision up to you.

"Never Be Afraid
To Enlist The Aid
of a Big And Powerful
Friend."

-Sachi

"Humans Hate To
Be Ignored, Which Makes
This A Powerful Tool.
But Don't Overuse It.
You'll Probably
Forget Why You Started
And Just Fall Asleep."

-*Notorious KAT*

"For Centuries,
Cats Have Been
A Never-Ending
Source Of Wisdom
and Entertainment"

-*Great Aunt
Winifred*

"Embrace
The Melting Pot."

-Great Uncle
Rufus

"Never
Let Life Put You
On A Leash."

-Tommy "Tom-Tom"
Thompson

"Try Not To Think
Too Much Of Yourself
- Even If You Look
Like Me."

-Gorgeous George

"There's No Such Thing As A Natural Enemy."

-Smokey the Cafe' Cat

"Sometimes I Like To Pretend I'm Meditating When I'm Just Taking a Well-Deserved Nap."

-*Snowy Paws Jinxy*

**Let A Little Art
Lighten Your Life.**

"He Travels Happiest
Who Travels
With a Friend."

-Angel "Miao"
Columbus

"Sometimes, I
Like To Be Alone With
My Thoughts"

*-Immanuel Kat*

"Humans Aren't
Stupid;
They Just Don't
Always Listen."

-Felicity
Hogbottom

# Advice to Kitten

You've got to love a human,
And give them lots of care.
They have no fur to warm them.
Poor things have only hair.

They never get sufficient sleep
And think eight hours will do.
This only makes them nervous
wrecks,
And keeps them feeling blue.

Find yourself a human;
Brighten up their day.
Let them pet and care for you
And teach them how to play.

- Miss Kitty

"Feeling A Little Nervous?
Try Sleeping With a Friend. "
(By Sleeping, I Mean Sleeping.)

-*Prudence*

"Cats will outsmart dogs
every time."
- John Grogan

"Do you hear that, Mr. Woofs?"
- Miss Kitty

"Life is a Team Effort.
One Face Washes The
Other."

-Fluffy and
Twinkles

"You can keep a dog; but it is the cat who keeps people, because cats find humans useful domestic animals."

- George Mikes

"You humans are pretty darned cute, big, but cute." - Miss Kitty

"This is The Only
Proper Way to
Headbutt A Friend."

-*Missy & Rufus*

"A Cat can purr its way out of anything."
- Donna McCrohan

"Let people know when you're happy." - Miss Kitty

I AM HAPPY BECAUSE EVERY ONE LOVES ME.

## "Life is All About Attitude"

### -Miss Kitty

## Pretend That You Don't Care

If a mouse escapes your clutches,
pretend that you don't care.
If you slide upon the throw rug,
pretend that you don't care.

If you break a cup or saucer,
spill the stew upon the floor,
the best advice that I can give you;
pretend that you don't care.

- Miss Kitty

"Cats are not loners.
We're just particular in choosing
our friends.

And we're not as needy as that other
species people keep as "pets".

You know who I'm talking about,
Mr. Woofs."

- Miss Kitty

"Cats seem to go on the principle that it never does any harm to ask for what you want."

- Joseph Wood Krutch

"Yet another thing humans can learn from cats." - Miss Kitty

("Miss Kitty, you are getting insufferable." - Jonny K.)

"My Grandparents
Tended The Land.
Take Pride in Your Roots."

-Clara Gardener

# Word to the Wise

"Having a bunch of cats around is good.
If you're feeling bad, just look at the cats,
you'll feel better, because they know
that everything is, just as it is."

— **Charles Bukowski**

"Life goes on; groove with it."

— Miss Kitty

Meet Our Editor...
Les S. Moore.
He doesn't Look
Frightening, But He
Can't Keep His Paws
Off The Delete Key.

*-Miss Kitty & Jonny K.*

"My Protégé, Sheba.
Probably Dreaming
Up A Brilliant Idea For
Her Own Book."

-Miss Kitty

As you might notice, Miss Kitty is especially fond of the works of Louis Wain. These pictures, as well as all the other images in the book, are in the public domain.

The editors would like to thank the

following websites

Wikimedia Commons

Pixbay.com

RawPixels.com

Pexels.com

We hope you enjoyed

our book.


If you did, please leave a review.

These matter more than you might think.


If you would like to write to Miss Kitty, please
send an email to her editor at:

OldTownPublishing@gmail.com

(Miss Kitty loves getting mail.)

(So does Jonny.)


OldTownPublishing.com